a frying pan
&
the apple core

Emily Ching

FACE TO FACE PRESS
NEW YORK

Copyright © Emily Ching, 2002

Published by Face to Face Press, 16 West 32nd Street,
Suite 10A, New York, New York 10001

All rights reserved. No part of this publication may be
reproduced or transmitted in any form or by any means,
electronic or mechanical, including photocopying, recording,
or any information storage and retrieval system, without
permission in writing from the publisher.

Bulk discounts available. Please contact the publisher.

Cover Design by TLC Graphics

Library of Congress Control Number: 99-69188

ISBN 1-929712-00-6

Printed in Canada by Hignell Book Printing.

First Edition, July 2002

10 9 8 7 6 5 4 3 2 1

a Frying Pan & the Apple Core

This tale is dedicated to my mother
and my brother with special thanks
to Opal Palmer Adisa for guiding me
through this process.

Foreword

Emily Ching cooks some mean art. It's funny, powerful, and solid, without ever pretending to be anything more or less than what it is. Like the old Dramatics line, and like Emily herself, what you see is what you get.

Her personal narratives form a seeking, always honest, sometimes wacky exploration of what it means to be a woman in this country. Except "a woman" is "this woman"—angry, comical, lonely, whimsical, black, white—fill in the blank here. That's Emily. Take it or leave it. That's what I've always liked about her work. She can hit the fierce topic—race, gender, class—without ever losing her smile or perspective.

Emily has that rare combination of being able to take her work seriously without taking herself too seriously. And in a world of self-important artists (redundant, I know) eager to crown themselves the next-greatest-thing-ever, that's a refreshing point of view. I'll never forget her hilarious senior portraits dressed up as Shirley Temple (Black), her childhood hero, preening and posing for the camera without inhibition. Even as I felt the pain of the once little girl struggling to identify with a role model she could never hope to be, I was still laughing. The Good Ship Lollipop has never been the same.

My Emily Ching experience began in 1992. It was my first quarter teaching at UCSB and halfway through my twenty-seventh year. She asked, in that point blank way of hers, if she could do an Independent Study with me.

I said yes. I agreed for several reasons. First, I was a rookie faculty and just plain didn't know any better. I learned quickly that Independent Studies often doubled as catch-all's—useful tools for savvy students avoiding difficult upper-division classes or maneuvering around scheduling conflicts caused by other classes, work, or their own poor planning. Whether this was the case with Emily or not, I'm still not quite sure. It certainly was when I was an undergraduate, but I kind of figured they would have fixed these types of things by now. Second, I wondered if Emily might have specifically sought me out because of our shared Chinese ancestry (her last name being Ching and all) and thought it might seem a bit callous or even culturally insensitive for me to disregard such an open outreach. I mean who was I to turn down a sister? When I got to know her well enough to ask, I found out her last name was actually acquired—adopted by her father after the *I Ching*. That was a new one. Finally, and most importantly, Emily was only the second Black student I had encountered on a campus of roughly 18,000. That was reason enough to go ahead. I later learned that she, like myself, identified as multiracial, and that this was our real shared ancestry—an ancestry familiar to anyone navigating the endless idiocies of job application questionnaires and what-are-you questions. A shared experience of explanation and second glances. Sure, maybe on campus she could be Black and I could be Asian. But in other, more familiar communities we were not quite. Plain and simple.

That's funny … you don't look _____.

Ten years later I was approached to write this foreword. Now in my thirty-seventh year, I was happy to find some good things didn't change. Like the sassy undergraduate who once told me I gave her the lowest grade she ever got as an Art Major (it was a B), Emily has lost none of her fire or honesty. She's just gotten more efficient.

A Frying Pan & The Apple Core pulls no punches with some difficult subject matter, yet it still manages to move lightly and with a deft touch. You can go into her world at your own pace and leave on your own accord. It's self-paced exercise with optional contact sparring. Internet traffic school. You can get hit if you want, and hit hard —but only if you want to be. No hard feelings. Call it a collection of poetry or prose, visual art or performance, education or activism. The work, like Emily, doesn't fit neatly into boxes and resists being defined. I know Emily wouldn't bother trying to explain, so what's the point of us struggling? It's just art. Step up and take a taste. (And if you've found the real thing, it's the best thing yet.)

Kip Fulbeck, Santa Barbara

Performance and video artist Kip Fulbeck is the author of Paper Bullets: A Fictional Autobiography, University of Washington Press (www.redsushi.com)

a frying pan...

When my father, Clarence, was two years old he started school. A skinny Black boy, whose sister was too scared to walk to kindergarten by herself. So he went with her.

Look, listen, and learn

Look, listen, and learn,

If you listen you will learn

But first you have to learn to listen.

...& the apple core

a frying pan...

Whenever he would find it fit, my father would speak at me for hours on end, repeating this little proverb he learned that first year in school.

This meant that I was to sit opposite him cross-legged, back straight, looking him in the face. By the time I reached junior high, I found an empty space two inches between his ear and his shoulder. As long as I stared there he didn't question my gaze.

I STARTED SCHOOL WHEN I WAS TWO,

BECAUSE MY SISTER WAS SCARED TO GO ALONE.

SHE WAS FIVE.

I know. I know you're smart.

We're smart. We're better than all of this. So why do I have to keep looking at you?

His eyes were somewhere between a jaundiced yellow and a rotting brown. Some people called them gold or hazel. His left eye was smaller than the other, bordered by a ragged scar on the fleshy part beneath his brow. Deep creases ran down the centers of his cheeks. His teeth were big and strong, stained with tar and smoke. He had those bumps on his face where he shaved, like other Black men.

...& the apple core

a frying pan...

> *THEY'RE TRYING TO GET ME.*
>
> *THEY CAN STRIKE THREE TIMES,*
>
> *THREE TIMES, THEN I HIT THEM BACK.*
>
> *I'M WEAK NOW,*
>
> *BUT I'LL HIT'EM BACK.*

He always spat on me and his West Indian accent came back when he got excited. When I wiped my face and looked disgusted he'd back up or stand and pace. Sometimes he'd get up to light his cigarette at the stove and I'd get a chance to slump or close my eyes or make faces at the wall. Usually I would flip the bird in his direction, showing my defiance and strength.

When you were a baby I had this dream.

They were after me, and they could fly,

and you could too.

You saved me.

You could fly, too, and you saved me.

I was tired of being Jesus Christ.

...& the apple core

a frying pan...

and sitting up straight. Tired of living under the specter of my mother's mythical family—some horrible Jews who were after him, because he was the only thing that stood between them and us.

Your mother's grandmother

made a fist at me in the doorway

and wouldn't let me in

unless I ate some of her food.

But I knew.

She didn't know that I knew, but I did.

I knew she was trying to put a spell on me.

So I told that old woman to fuck off.

...& the apple core

a frying pan...

I am named after my great-grandmother. She came to America by herself when she was nine or eight or thirteen. All the way from Russia. She got pneumonia while she was on a train (in Mexico? or Amsterdam? or was it France?). She almost died, but someone helped.

SHE CAME TO LIVE IN NEW YORK WITH HER SISTER.

SO I KILLED THE BITCH.

...& the apple core

a frying pan...

She came to us one night while we were sleeping.

So I said to myself,

"I'll take this bitch places she don't wanna go."

I went down to Chinatown

and to the skankiest places I knew.

To strip joints and bars, to places

where men were kissing other men,

and down alleys where bad shit was going on.

I took her places she never should've seen.

And it killed her.

And I told your mother that I killed her.

The next morning she got a call that she was dead.

Didn't you, Natalie?

YOU CAN ASK YOUR MOTHER IF IT'S TRUE.

My mother's grandmother Anna died while my mom was pregnant with me. My mom never told her about me, but she says that she saw her ghost once. Anna smiled at her, approvingly. So when my mother dreamed she had a little girl named Emi

...& the apple core

a frying pan...

> I had a dream once that I met Anna,
>
> but last year I saw a picture of her
>
> and it was a different woman.

...& the apple core

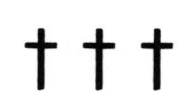

a frying pan...

> *LOOK, LISTEN, AND LEARN*
>
> *HOW CAN YOU LISTEN IF YOU HAVEN'T LEARNED TO LOOK?*

He usually chose to yell at us between 7 and 8 p.m. Late enough to keep me awake until 2 in the morning, but too early to have done much more than eat dinner and think about doing my homework. It almost always started while I was watching TV, lying down and way too close to the screen.

...& the apple core

a frying pan...

YOU'RE GONNA END UP LIKE YOUR MOTHER.

You're gonna end up with glasses like your mother.

Lying down that close to the TV

is gonna ruin you eyes.

Just like reading while you're on your back.

I had to wear glasses when I was your age.

I know.

I had to train my eyes to get better.

Do you see me lying down?

Fuckin' sit up.

...& the apple core

a frying pan...

In eighth grade, I failed the vision test.

I told my mom, but it was the same year that Haley's Comet came. I could see the comet. I could even see the tail.

So she said there was no way a girl who could see the tail of Haley's Comet with her plain eyes could need glasses.

I sat up front in my classes and memorized the colors my friends were wearing until I was a sophomore in high school.

WHY ARE YOU WATCHING THAT SHIT?

NATALIE,

...& the apple core

a frying pan...

What the fuck are these kids watching? Do you need a laugh track to tell you when something's funny? They're trying to brainwash you. If it's funny they wouldn't need a laugh track.

Natalie, why are they watching that shit?

Me and my little brother always had to watch our favorite shows on the sly. If we got caught watching "Different Strokes" or "The Facts of Life" or even "Good Times" (in re-runs), and if he was in the mood, he'd shut it off and we all caught it. His lectures lasted a few hours, until Leelo fell asleep.

Then my mom and I sat there until it was late enough for me to feign fatigue.

He always ordered my mother to take off her glasses while we sat there.

...& the apple core

a frying pan...

I used to think she was lucky,

because she didn't really have to look at him.

It didn't occur to me how powerless

a blind woman can feel.

When she'd take me to bed, I always asked why we didn't leave or told her to stay with me in my room so he couldn't get her. I fought visions that ended in bruises, in a permanent lump on the top of her head, and I cried extra hard. I was scared and I wanted to make her feel bad enough that she might stay.

But it never worked.

...& the apple core

a frying pan...

Softly, she told me to shut up,

she would come back later.

So I lay there.

Alert.

Listening.

Waiting.

Ready to pop up and be there when she really

needed me.

                                      Ready to protect her.

Ready to stop his blows with my presence,

with my witnessing glare.

But I only cried until I passed out or it was quiet.

Sometimes the sound of a shower running

at 4 a.m. told me it was over for a little while.

As she washed him away

...& the apple core

a frying pan...

I fell asleep.

...& the apple core

† † †

a frying pan...

My first county fair was in Ventura.

I was five and I got to ride the Ferris wheel. Just the thought of a roller-coaster made me sick. The fairgrounds were next to the beach and filled with surfers, farmers, homeboys, the rich, and the poor.

My mom told me that all the carnies were drug addicts and nasty people. Her friend Terrie told her so, and she was a part-time carnie herself. She said all the games were rigged, so I never played and never got to win a cheap stuffed snake or teddy bear.

...& the apple core

a frying pan...

I liked the big pink cotton candy and my mom gave me a bite of her corn dog that wasn't a dog at all but a big chunk of cheese.

FINE YOU BITCHES STAY THEN.

My dad wanted to go.

He never liked crowds and thought fairs were a waste of money anyway. I knew it was over. I hadn't even seen the miniature pony or walked the full stretch of the midway.

For some reason, (maybe it was my popped out bottom lip or maybe she felt a little crazy), my mom said no.

She said no.

...& the apple core

a frying pan...

We weren't leaving.

I must have been a sight then—popped-out lip, eyes as big as coconuts, and a little pink tongue just resting there in a mouth wide with surprise.

FINE! YOU BITCHES STAY THEN.

And my mom and I walked away. Just me and my mom. My hand was small and chubby in hers and I knew my dad was wrong.

He called me a bitch.

He said you bitches.

Plural.

...& the apple core

a frying pan...

When I was eight, and eleven, and sixteen,

I reminded him. You said bitches at the fair.

You called <u>me</u> a bitch. When I was five, at the

fair.

And he looked at me, dismissing it. But I knew.

I remembered.

He called me a bitch when I was five at the fair.

...& the apple core

† † †

a frying pan...

I USED TO RUN FULL SPEED WITH YOU ON MY SHOULDERS,

WHEN WE LIVED BACK IN L.A.

YOU WERE TOUGH.

YOU HELD ON TO MY 'FRO AND MY EARS.

I WAS WEARING THOSE HIGH-HEELED BOOTS,

AND YOU'D PULL OUT BIG CHUNKS OF MY HAIR.

BIG PATCHES.

YOU NEVER LET GO.

...& the apple core

a frying pan...

My father had two tactics.

Scream until his voice went out and blame my mother for the disintegration of everything; or re-tell the same sugar sweet stories of the days when he and I were friends. These reminiscences ended in his tears for dramatic flair.

YOU USED TO LIKE ME.

My father thrived on the memories of the days before we moved to Ventura. When we lived as a family, so to speak. We left Los Angeles when I was four.

Only a handful of photographs remain indicating that what he remembers might have been true. They are pictures of a small musky-yellow apartment on Kingsley, with a full-length mirror, a corduroy bean bag, and a miniature kitchen set I got for Christmas.

A blue plastic pool with a built-in slide and a shimmering gold Cadillac were both parked in the driveway. The Cadillac was repossessed when my mother declared bankruptcy in '77.

...& the apple core

a frying pan...

WE WERE GOOD BUDDIES.

I WORKED NIGHTS, AND YOU'D WAKE UP

WHEN I GOT HOME,

BEFORE I EVEN GOT TO THE DOOR.

YOU'D BE WAITING FOR ME.

YOU AND ME WERE TIGHT.

Waiting.

I always waited . . .

for things to change in the house when he got home. For the television banter and chatter of harmless bickering to turn into booming Jimi Hendrix and the silent tension of tender eggshells.

...& the apple core

a frying pan...

At sixteen I had a best friend and my first boyfriend to spend nights with on the phone. I relished the time I could excuse myself from my family and hide in my bedroom, talking for hours. My record was a sixteen-hour conversation with three bathroom breaks and a half hour for dinner. In my room, the voices outside became hollow and distant.

Things were sort of okay.

...& the apple core

† † †

a frying pan...

CAN I LIGHT MY CIGARETTE?

Seventeen years of anger and frustration balled up into five hard slams of my mother's fake Teflon frying pan to the back of his skull, and my father asked me if he could light his cigarette.

Calmly.

And that was all. It was over.

...& the apple core

a frying pan...

Any hope that the persistent pulse of anger searching its way through each nerve, vessel, and vein of my body—any hope of that pulse leaving me was dashed.

                              Pfft.

Try as I may, my father gave me that one thing.

That throb. That pulse.

No frying pan or apple core

could make that anger go.

...& the apple core

a frying pan...

One other time I watched it come close.

304 West Ramona Street.

My father closed his gaping mouth

over a red delicious apple,

in the midst of yelling.

It refused to go down and it refused to come up.

It just stopped him.

Silent.

My small brother, my mother, and my nine-year-old eyes stared at him.

Silent.

Waiting for the apple to fix things. Keep him silent and unarmed.

I glanced at my mother, wondering if it was real or if she would stand up and wrap her strong baby-carrying arms around his chest and squeeze from behind.

But we all stayed still.

...& the apple core

a frying pan...

Silent.

Waiting for the red delicious apple to save us.

Just waiting.

My father's belly rippled and his chest heaved just a little. It wasn't that dreadful or scary. It was almost peaceful and slow.

KUH HUUUH.

I heard the skin rip a little

as the apple went down.

Me and the core,

defeated.

...& the apple core

a frying pan...

LOOK AT ME WHEN I'M TALKING TO YOU!

                                          I'm looking.

Your skin is sagging a little more than it did when I was nine. You grind your teeth more often and I crack my neck in the same twist and jar you've done for years.

                            I'm looking at you
and I don't see any of this ending.

I weighed more than my father when I was seventeen. He was stronger. But he loved me. He loved me so he wouldn't hit back, despite the frying pan. I was seventeen, so they couldn't put me away for that long. I was already put away.

> When he went to light his cigarette,
> he lit it on the stove.

Always on the stove. No matches or sweet smelling silver lighter since 304 West Ramona Street.

> When he lit his home-rolled Drum cigarette,
> he lit it on the stove.

...& the apple core

a frying pan...

With his back turned.

I heard him tell my brother,

WE DON'T NEED ANY FUCKING HAND-ME-DOWNS.

HEY, LEELO COME HELP ME TEAR THIS SHIT UP.

WE DON'T NEED ANYBODY ELSE'S FUNK IN THIS HOUSE.

It took less than two hours for the two of them to completely destroy the couch my mother's boss had given us. For two semi-blissful months we had owned a dining room table, four shiny metal and brown vinyl dining room chairs, and a long brown and tan plaid sofa that held me from head to toe.

We put the table in the dining room where my dad slept, with the chairs and sofa clustered around the television. For a little while it almost looked like a real home.

It was my fault the couch got thrown away. When my father came out of the bathroom, he found me lying down on the couch watching cartoons.

What are you doing there, lying

your head on somebody else's shit?

You think that's cool, fucking your eyes up,

with your head all up in some stranger's dirt?

What the fuck is this Natalie?"

...& the apple core

a frying pan...

By the middle of that Saturday afternoon, I sat up cross-legged on the floor staring at old reruns of "Happy Days." I tried to forget that the men of the house were downstairs ripping apart one of the only relics of civilization my family owned.

I tried to erase my mother's "I-knew-it-would-happen-sooner-or-later-but-why-did-you-have-to-lie-down-on-it-when-he-was-home" face from the TV screen.

A few months later, I could only use the heavy dining room chairs to pin him against the stove

...& the apple core

a frying pan...

With his back turned, just asking for it.

...& the apple core

† † †

a frying pan...

During the last year, nothing was left in the small dining area where my father slept and lived, except a yellow beaten copy of the "I Ching" (the edition with Jung's preface), three pennies, and a neatly rolled pile of $8.99 Kmart blankets in faded blues, yellows, and pinks.

On the bar that separated his room from the kitchen, he kept a bag of Drum tobacco and a white package of Zig Zag papers with metallic writing. On some occasions there might be a pad of 11 X 14 bleached-white drawing paper with a black fountain pen, or maybe a copy of *Muscle and Fitness* magazine.

...& the apple core

a frying pan...

He kept his clothes in the hall linen closet; his important papers in a cabinet above the refrigerator; and his brown dress boots and white hurraches by the door.

You don't need to traipse dirt all over the house.

Your mother doesn't have a vacuum cleaner.

Besides, pretend you're gonna stay awhile.

Pretend you like us.

My father was obsessed with the notion that our apartment wasn't really ours to do with as we pleased. For this reason there were no pictures or shelves on the walls and we were not allowed to wear shoes inside. When things spilled they were immediately tended to, for fear that a stain on the rug would jeopardize the security deposit or look bad when the housing authorities came through for their periodic inspections.

...& the apple core

a frying pan...

The last three years that my father lived with us, he went without a job. But on the morning of every HUD inspection he woke up early, put on his white Levi jacket and came back at nightfall.

HEY, COME HERE! CHECK THIS SHIT OUT.

YOU'RE GONNA LIKE THIS.

THIS IS BA-A-A-AD. TELL ME WHAT YOU THINK.

The only time my father seemed content was while he painted on his brown '78 Dodge Charger.

Always outside when I got off the bus from school, he called me over to the garage to check out the new section he painted on the hood. Bright yellows, reds, and oranges or metallic blues, silvers, and greens. He used model paints and tiny brushes to transform his barely running, gutted-for-speed automobile into what he called his "masta-piece" but what I considered a disgusting embarrassment.

HEY, CHECK THIS OUT. THIS IS COOL, YOU LIKE IT?

I responded to his wide, yellow grin with a wrinkled forehead and a twisted-lipped,

> "There's a naked lady on it."

...& the apple core

a frying pan...

You don't like anything I do.

Just wait. If somebody was gonna pay 10 grand for this car, you'd like it then, huh?

You'd fuckin' like it then.

You just wait. . .

I'd hear his muttering as I walked upstairs, sure that no one would ever offer him 10 grand for that broken-down piece of shit.

No one would offer him anything.

Two days before we dropped my dad off at the beach up the freeway, his masterpiece was towed to Norm's Auto Salvage.

We drove my '90 Festiva to edge of Ventura County the day we said good-bye.

...& the apple core

a frying pan...

> *I GUESS I CAN'T SMOKE IN HERE, HUH?*
>
> *CAN I AT LEAST USE THE LIGHTER?*

A hollowed 50-year-old Black man could not smoke his cigarette in my new car. No matter how much my mother's glare pleaded from the back seat in my rear-view mirror.

It was my car. I was kind to let him sit up front with me. The executioner can only show so much mercy and survive the killing.

It was the last drive the four of us took

to the rocks where the ocean

met the freeway.

I was driving and this time

there would be no yelling.

For once, it was calm.

So THIS IS IT. . . THIS IS IT.

...& the apple core

a frying pan...

My mother, my brother, and I stood in front of the car while he faced us carrying his Kmart blankets wrapped around a change of clothes.

Boy, I sure did raise you guys strong.

Musta done something right,

the way the three of you are facing me.

United, huh?

I could feel the sea soaked wind on my face and the slow perspiration where my arm brushed against my mother. It was overcast and so tragically romantic I couldn't help but smile.

Neither could he, as he came a little closer.

EMILY,

...& the apple core

a frying pan...

> *YOU BETTER TAKE CARE OF YOUR MOTHER.*
>
> *AND YOU, LEELO, YOU BETTER WATCH OUT FOR YOUR SISTER.*
>
> *AAHH. . . I*
>
> *GUESS I DON'T HAVE TO WORRY. I . . .*
>
> *YOUR MOTHER RAISED YOU GUYS PRETTY GOOD, HUH?*

Serious as a judge.

Serious

as a judge.

I always lost at that game. I always cracked the smile. Except for my mom, I could always get her by sticking out my curled up "taco tongue."

He never lost, no matter how stoned.

One last time. Serious as a judge.

WELL, I GUESS I BETTER GO.

...& the apple core

a frying pan...

HEY,

THANKS FOR THE RIDE.

Three of us got in my car.

My mother riding shot gun.

...& the apple core

a frying pan...

My father became little in the distance.

I cried the whole way home.

...& the apple core

†††

Face to Face Press is an independent community press devoted to publishing all genres of written works that explore the mixed race, interracial, transracial, and multicultural experience. The press seeks to build coalitions across marginalized communities; give underrepresented writers a forum for expression and access into the publishing industry; and advocate that communities of color create and maintain their own media.

Face to Face Press
16 West 32nd Street, Ste 10A
New York New York 10001
tel 212.494.9143
fax 419.828.4684
publisher@face2facepress.com
http://www.face2facepress.com

OTHER TITLES BY <u>FACE TO FACE</u>

REDEMPTION by Emma Farry, ISBN 1-929712-03-0, $14.95, 232 pages, Trade Softcover, April 2002

REDEMPTION chronicles the life of Solomon Cortesi as seen through the eyes of three women. These women propel Solomon on a journey of self-discovery that spans generations and reveals to him powerful revelations about a curse that has plagued his family for more than a century. What he ultimately discovers sets him free to find a path leading to understanding and forgiveness.

VOICES OF BROOKLYN: WRITINGS FROM THE WOMEN OF COLOR WRITERS' WORKSHOP, ISBN 1-929712-01-4, $6.00, 110 pages, Illus., Trade Softcover, September 2000

VOICES OF BROOKLYN features the poetry, prose, and short stories of 14 women of color who sought a creative written and spoken word forum for their voices.

ORDER FORM:

REDEMPTION by Emma Farry, 1-929712-03-0, $14.95, April 2002

VOICES OF BROOKLYN: WRITINGS FROM THE WOMEN OF COLOR WRITERS' WORKSHOP, 1-929712-01-4, $6.00, September 2000

FREE SHIPPING! Please send me:

_____ copies of REDEMPTION ($14.95/book)
_____ copies of VOICES ($6.00/book)
(8.25% sales tax will be added for NY & CT residents).
I have enclosed a: ☐ check, ☐ money order, or
☐ cashiers check payment made out to: FACE to FACE Press, 16 West 32nd St, Ste 10A, NY, NY 10001

Mailing Address:

Name _____

Address _____

_____

Tel _____

Email _____

or for secure online ordering visit:
www.face2facepress.com or amazon.com.

Questions or Comments? Contact us:
tel 212-494-9142; fax 419-828-4684;
email publisher@face2facepress.com

Wholesale Distribution: Baker & Taylor